Quicksand Beach

KATE BINGHAM
Quicksand Beach

seren

Seren is the book imprint of
Poetry Wales Press Ltd
57 Nolton Street, Bridgend, Wales, CF31 3AE
www.seren-books.com

ISBN 1-85411-411-5

A CIP record for this title is available from the British Library.

The publisher acknowledges the financial assistance
of the Welsh Books Council.

Printed in Hoefler by Bell & Bain Ltd, Glasgow

Cover image: Surfers – cotton
by the Calico Printers Association, England 1937
© V&A Images/Victoria and Albert Museum

Contents

Mediterraneo

Lunch at the Italian with Mum
so proud of my belly
she's catching eyes with everyone
and ordering too much food.
The waiter predicts my date.
The maitre d' says you will be a girl
and soon, before I know it, all grown up
and having a baby of your own
and it will be my turn to pay
and if we come back then he promises
dessert for free. Mum grins expectantly
as I re-read the menu and your left heel
kicks twice for chocolate mousse.

Diamonds

Let's not have an argument this year
about my birthday. You know what I want
because you always ask and always spoil
it by then not giving me diamonds,
choosing some less extravagant present
to symbolise the extent of your love -

orchids that die, a hat I'll only love
while it's in fashion, useful shoes. Each year
I try my best to want the very present
you wanted to give when really I want
you to want to give me diamonds
which stay in style and never spoil.

Where I come from it's traditional to spoil
the birthday girl, indulge her like a loved
child whether you disapprove of diamonds
dug up and traded year after year
to finance wars only despots could want
instead of food for those they represent

or not. But you seem to resent present
giving. Maybe my expectation spoils
spontaneity and makes you want
not to give anything, believing love
should be its own reward. Maybe the year
I manage not to mention diamonds,

even in jest, I'll get them: diamonds
you've waited a decade to present,
mine all along but for the asking, years
of petulance now threatening to spoil
the moment I accept your token of love,
its leather box leaving me nothing to want.

Or maybe you're right: I don't know what I want
and only out of spite say diamonds,
wanting the argument, a measure of love
superior to any birthday present.
But let's not have an argument and spoil
this celebration of my thirtieth year,

my birthday. Next year for sure I'll want
you to spoil me, please, with diamonds
but for the present I'll make do with love.

Eighteenth

There was a craze for fountain pens.
Fat lacquered ones, walnut-effect, gold-nibbed,
unlocked and lifted, two-handed,
from spot-lit glass cabinets and carried over plush
by silent nail-varnished assistants
to the desk where you and your mum or dad
would have been waiting almost eighteen years,
not talking much, you worrying because the pen
you liked best was also the most expensive.
We kept their pass-the-parcel packaging,
treasured for months the slippery, important plastic bag,
the velvety plump moulded to fit our pen alone,
room underneath for two free cartridges
and an instruction manual in fourteen languages, ours first,
the twelve-month guarantee, as if a pen could break down,
when what we liked best was its low-tech simplicity,
that we could want a thing invented centuries before,
that it could symbolise our coming of age.
We scribbled in sepia, wrote everyone cheques
for a million hazelnuts. On birthdays
we'd crowd into the library at lunch
and watch the tip of a new pen touch its first white sheet,
the hand behind solemn and quivering, unsure
whether to doodle or draw or let the nib
try for itself, licking the page in thirsty blue-black stripes
as if it knew this was the end of freedom
and that soon it would have twisted to accommodate
each hesitation, dot and loop, its every molecule
straining with something like love as I leaned in,
imagining a future shaped by neat italics
where whatever I wanted I need only write it down.

Paradise

It's a rich man's world and yesterday
I married him despite what mother said
about love, the only luxury
I never wanted to afford. Instead
the Caribbean, islands to swim from
and my own solicitous white sand
he promises. He knows about women
and sulphur. I can have all of Iceland.
Regular sunsets. The tailfeather
from a bird of paradise on the path
to the bungalow where fairweather
wives live with the poolboy. Already my heart
wishes for less. A pomegranate seed
with the light in it is happiness.
Jaguars asleep on the stairway sneeze
if I so much as think of his caress.

The Island-designing Competition

starts with two blank sheets and a box of pencils
sharpened by Dad with a carving-knife.
We hunch at the table, squiggling headlands,
inlets, estuaries, then filling in the ground between
with swamps and volcanoes, rainforest, glaciers, a ski-resort.
It has to be imaginative and plausible,
needs water, for instance, dungeons and schools
and villages with names like Hiccupbottom, Lurch,
Thornton-le-Spam. By lunch, my brother
has moved on to climate: his palm trees lean north,
his capital springs shanties in the aftermath
of last year's hurricane, and every bus-stop
harbours a scarlet dhow – for when there are floods,
his key explains. *Any excuse to draw a boat,*
I mutter, snatching the red for my stick men,
each to represent one hundred votes.
They stand in public squares demanding a recount
as the President mouths his acceptance speech
and such is the confusion no one sees
my brother's auxiliary fleet
tack past the mustard and salt and strawberry jam
and on through international waters,
gathering, now, in battle formation
half a league south of Quicksand Beach.

Highnam Court Violin Camp, 1981

Four hours of Orchestra in the ballroom every day
and, after supper, music for fun
like madrigals, or rounds, or string quartets,
or everyone stand in a semi-circle making up claps.
In a single week I learned 'erection',
page one of the score of Rite of Spring
and how to pop corn. I learned to balloon debate
and never again choose politician.
After the riots, people were saying
the country needed a Royal Wedding to put it in harmony.
I sat on a bench in the telly room
not following Jeremy Morris, my love, all afternoon.
That night there was a barbecue
and I ate twenty-six plums. My new best friend,
the Vivaldi soloist, fell through duckweed
jumping across the watergarden in her concert shoes
and cried because her mum would know
she hadn't been practising. The Beethoven went too fast
so they sent me to lead the juniors
for Bartok's Hungarian Folk Dances instead
and I still wish we had not had to start again
in front of so many parents.

Roads

I

Endless motorways. The mysterious
backward caress of street-lights quietly
wiping our blankets and best pyjamas,
even our hands, until we believed that soft
insidious brown must be the colour
of boredom itself and, momentarily
distracted by the thought that itchiness
could have a colour too, forgot to ask
for the umpteenth time *Are we nearly there?*
This much our childhoods had in common:
pins and needles, bickering front seat and back,
crumbs in the ashtray, games we can play
half asleep with our heads on the window,
the signposts' arabic looming blue.

II

I have a motorway of my own:
a hundred miles of white-lined, cat-eyed
quality tarmac, cambered to perfection
by the country's finest engineers
and far from anywhere you'd want to go.
Six service stations, two hard shoulders
and a central reservation scented
and yellow with gorse the summer through.
I love to walk it in zigzags, cartwheel,
hop or pigeon-step from light to light,
or sometimes idle on the verge
rewriting the Highway Code and ringing in
hoax emergencies, or flick through Loot
pretending I might buy myself a car.

III

A romantic spot it was and your question
not unexpected. Arm in arm
we walked down the hill to your mum's house,
sat quietly through beef on the bone
and the rest of that long sunny Sunday afternoon
and could not look each other in the eye.
You slept on the lawn. I read a magazine.
My turn to drive. Still shy, we played I-spy
in the dark: something beginning with me
in a chilly white dress at the back of the church,
balloons on string in the pony field
and five thousand Audis waiting to park.
An usher who won't wear his buttonhole
sits on the gate whistling Mendelssohn.

I V

And now it's your turn to be annoyed:
joining the motorway with an empty tank
when physics and economy suggest
it's better to fill up first on a slow road.
At services I climb out after you
and hang about in ugly strip-light
holding the petrol cap as if to help us
be quicker, but thirty miles on
you are still calculating how much time
we could have saved, as if we'd have been home
by now, unpacked, undressed, asleep
or even – think of it – so far ahead
we're already finishing breakfast.
Kiss me good-bye, remember your briefcase.

V

We reached the moors at 2 a.m. No phone,
no farm, no services, abandoned HGVs
and every traveller with sense at home
asleep, the country revelling in Christmas freeze,
black ice on silent motorways. You drove,
I watched the road, I watched the baby breathe.
Not turning back, even then, it seemed as though
you forgot the numb hillside, risking our lives
to please some irresistible whim or dare,
but if I ask you now I know you'll say
it wasn't that dangerous, we'd come so far,
we were so nearly there. Scare me again,
I never loved you more than when our car
span quietly across fresh snow in the fast lane.

6th December 1998

Your mouth is the start of a love affair
I have been planning ever since felt tip pen
disfigured my Goldilocks,

smudging the outline of her lips
and looping her cheek with forceps marks
which neither fairy liquid

nor two decades in the attic at home
can fade. My darling, yours
will disappear in days.

In the delivery room I cry because you are so rare,
so sure,
I hardly dare to touch or kiss you,

even to let you live, slithering
towards ill-health and accident with every second,
every breath.

Meanwhile, you've opened your mouth
as wide as you can
and here I am holding you anyway,

feeling your bottom lip
curl under my salty nipple and your tongue contract
like a heart-beat.

The Mouths of Babes

1. Sucking

Inside, your mouth is the shape
of a single perfectly accomplished gulp

but nothing can quench for long
the hour-before-breakfast saliva taste of well-chewed gum

when bi-planes have the high blue hemisphere to themselves
and postmen crunch on broken emeralds.

11. Tasting

In a previous existence this tongue
was the tongue of Columbus,
five times coarser,
sticky with Italian and Portuguese,
as silver and elastic as a hooked fish
pleading for ocean.

Saliva, its element, sealed each farewell
as he set sail
imagining the first tomato
crushed and bleeding like a sunset
week after week no closer,
swallowing his mouth's horizon.

Mariners wept on deck
and salt from the beard of the great adventurer
fell like hail,
a scatter of crystals
in the savage glittering Atlantic calm.

iii. Speaking

Harmonica and mumble
through the finger flavour of a weekday afternoon
accompanied by rain at the window
and the slosh of washing machine on bass,
your lichened buds wet babygrows
polishing the drum, so clotted with stodge
I taste like a voice on the phone
and the louder you hum the further off I seem –

you stretch like Wiener schnitzel,
wishing for the mouth of an anteater or frog.

Milk

What happens to the milk you leave for next time
when the next time you suck it will be formula
with me in another room chewing my nails?
I am so full the ducts rub like polystyrene balls
in a bean bag; my nipples burn. Eleven months on
I am as passionate as a new-born
but you just slide to the floor and crawl away,
each bedtime help yourself to less and less.
On top of me eight nights after our final feed,
your father crushes out the last of it –
a sugary seep across my ribs, so much
we have to change the sheet.

Superiority

It's been a joke so long now I think I must actually believe
in the superiority of women over men,
most women over men,
most men,
        at least where flexibility, attention to detail,
and strong communication skills come in, and it's true
we do crash fewer cars, murder less, rob less,
buy more books, more stuff, have better sex.

I think I must believe all this
because one night, just as your dad and I are falling asleep,
I ask if he ever wished he'd been a woman,
and when he says *No* I am amazed.

He never wished it could have been his belly,
his nipples ripening, his neck you'd nuzzle for sleepily?
Never looked at us, mother and child, and hated himself
                                        for a moment,
feeling his love become envy?
                        Not really, he smiles.
He closes his eyes, curls into me, holding my hands.
How like a man, I tell myself, to think
he's happy as he is.

Gale Force Ten

The wind wanted everything to be flat
so I lay down on the pavement
and by and by some leaves came tumbling along
with tissues, chip wrap, polystyrene snow
and a carrier bag of Persian blue
from the twenty-four hour milk shop.
What an assortment I collected,
just lying there in the way like a speed bump.
That morning alone I was responsible
for at least three bin-liners worth,
my body all that lay between them
and Hampstead Garden Suburb,
forty-eight junctions of the M1 motorway
and the arctic north.

Monogamy

I blame it on the backlash: free love
in the Eighties was for hippies, no one
liked Thatcher but monogamy
seemed more efficient, comforting to State
and individual alike, less last
resort than a celebration in bed

of the right to choose, not make your bed
and lie in it so much as a labour of love
we willingly fell in with, certain at last:
I wanted you, you wanted me. Alone
for the first time and in no fit state
for company we didn't see monogamy –

dumb, satisfied, unsung monogamy –
sneak in and slide between us on the bed,
backdating itself as if to reinstate
respectability, disguised as love's
romantic ideal and mocking our offhand, one
night stand bravado. It wants us to last,

our happiness, like a disease, its last
chance to spread – as if monogamy
transmits non-sexually from one
adoring couple to the next – to embed
itself in a world where pleasure and love
live separately and sit again in state,

pass sentence on what neither Church nor State
condemn outright. But what if we do last?
Time's not the test. Who loves best won't always love
longest, might not respect monogamy's
insistence, its assumption that all beds
must be forsaken but the one

one lies in in love. My eyes are for no one
but you, my love. We lie in a state
of easy innocence, a bed
of roses, tumbled and fragrant to the last
linen bud, but what's monogamy
without temptation, faith without love?

Therefore for love we should sacrifice one
thing alone: monogamy; maintain a state
of mutual jealousy, outlast our bed.

Breath

You never slept well. I'd rub your back, remember,
sit easily astride and knead exhaustion
deep into the skin between your tender
shoulder-blades, or when it was cold run just one
hand from side to side under the duvet,
the repetition hypnotising us both.
We had a single mattress on the floor, lay
anyhow, naked so close you took my breath
as now I worry I must be taking yours,
curled up beside you, too dazed to move.
I seem to get less generous in love
but you have learned to lie awake for hours
quietly motionless, letting me sleep.
At breakfast again insist you're happy.

Last Night

We thought it was rain, side by side
lay quietly below our midnight roof-light
listening to rapturous fat darts
batter the glass.

Children were jumping off tower blocks,
lighting candles, looting, having sex.
Parents remembered lullabies. Some held, some
smothered their young

rather than watch them die
slowly of hunger, cold, disease, or compromise
the quality of their own survival.
Husbands clutched wives

but you were exhausted, filled your ears
with cotton wool and took a pill, rolled over
away from me, cocooned in rumpled sheets,
determined to sleep

until morning, or whatever name
we'd find for when the sun has risen,
filtering through something like snow
on the window.

From the *Chronicles* of the Abbess of Almesbury

Three or more unremarkable days
in succession and they doubt again,
awkwardly, want back their thrown-away
possessions. Some I surprise in the lane
hitchhiking, poor souls, with carrier bags
for alibis, a sag of berries
to wave or nibble as they straggle
back for the night, chap-lipped and ill at ease.
Others plot in the refectory,
my downfall usually. I will be told
what troublemakers to expect
on which dank stair and, not too old
or womanly to fight, though woman
I am, would argument prefer to win
than war. I keep efficient spies. Happen
what may outside, good order within
will preserve us. The villagers butchered
a Tamworth with six eyes yesterday.
Spring tides: even the sand in the orchard
is black. Five apples on a single tree!
When I came here as a girl there were roads
everywhere. You could hear them roaring.
How easily people would come and go –
but I have promised to think no more
of the past. They are young and cannot bear
that I miss what I teach them to hate.
Only lions roar now, and still by law
we may not shoot at them. The climate
so alters no one will challenge, yet,
the conservationists but in a whisper.
Books kept secret for a hundred years
appear on the mountainside. O scavengers,
is there among you still a literate child?
Does she grow well in your better air?

Snow in May

I knew, but kept on having children
all the same, chose to prefer protracted
environmental degradation
to the world war mother expected
heavy with me and in her own way
wondering too how to explain why
that felt right. Each generation fancies
it might produce a saviour for the next,
but of my sons and daughters none can see
what's wrong with snow in May or the sex
of aphids, and the end of the world
drags on. At Christmas their father loves
to walk through woodland shooting at birds,
so I like to think we probably shan't starve.

Divorce

I had been looking forward to divorce –
recriminations, therapy and casual sex,
the disentangling of my life from yours

by sympathetic girl solicitors
who blush referring to you as my ex
and practice to avoid their own divorce.

I would have let you keep the chest of drawers
and hung my pants and socks on picture hooks
like bunting. What was mine would be not yours,

I'd cut my hair (too short) make common cause
with spinsters in wine-bars, bandy regrets
or shrug them off: you marry, death or divorce

come next, or so I thought. But love endures –
the mirror in the wardrobe door reflects
your face in mine and mine in yours,

a couple of fond baggy shameless bores
blessed with unmitigated happiness.
At night I wake from dreaming of divorce,
my arms and legs in sweat, tangled with yours.

Rooftop Car-park

I was a child again, standing with Mum
between parked cars and waiting
as usual for her to let me in,
not scared but apprehensive in the late
night supermarket rooftop car-park calm.
There had been rain. Purple-red clouds the size
of oil-tankers jammed the horizon
and the tarmac gleamed. Those were the days
of her worst life, when any small thing
could set her off and I'd be waiting
as usual for the next explosion
only now she wasn't a nail bomb
but a lion, leaping effortlessly
onto the bonnet and spitting at me.

The Lion

He wasn't my lion, you understand,
he just arrived, a stink in the kitchen,
ravenous, abandoned and scabby all over.
Waited quivering for me to drop the roast and run,
and when, as in a dream, I offered
Whiskas instead, lowered his head
and snarled at the cat's best tupperware.
Only an animal in pain, I thought,
would be so choosy, but when I pulled the thorn
from his torn paw still he refused to eat
and stood there needing someone to hurt,
my human cries to soothe his lion heart.

Nice

Our second day, at noon, a siren
rose from the stuccoed city, winding
off-key between palm-trees and peeling
balconies, calling us out to the garden
to see for ourselves no evidence
of smoke or panic, only blue skies,
and pleasure boats in the bay. Inside, our sense
of emergency dulled to unease:
me at the low sink rinsing tomatoes,
you on a stool to inspect the apartment's
yellow enamel boiler, wondering
if we should ring for a plumber,
or did it always hum like a bomb
in a war film falling through fire alarms?

Return

But then one sunny morning I tired of
café au lait and *broderie anglaise*
bedlinen and I could see I'd have
to go back. London was weak earl grey
and still in the grip of flood-warnings
no one knew whether to believe.
At night old men hid rowing boats up trees
and senior executives ate raw things
in riverside restaurants. I had had thieves –
a note in the rice read *more is less* –
but the police weren't interested. They tested
my breath for lies and checked my resumé:
three heartbreaks and a fine for covetously
wishing I had been my neighbour's wife.

Epilogue

It got so bad only the bankers could afford
to live in Central London, rampant wisteria
blossoming all summer long through razor wire
and everywhere the hum of bored, exhausted
cleaning ladies, gardeners and *au pairs*.
Winters too warm to justify the mink
I kept in case of revolution, never once wore
after the funeral. A decade stupid with drink
and other men. My name less and less spoken.
I sold the Residence when friends stopped asking
me to stand for election, but then
what else could I have done, wife of a king
who turns out not to have been dead after all,
just dozing in a cave somewhere in Cornwall?

His Eyes

Still learning to take his contact lenses out,
my love leans at the mirror pinching his eyes
into a bloodshot, swollen mess.

He never dreams, but drifts instead
between unfocused fantasy and the morning alarm,
not sure a wink of it took place in sleep.

Even now, as we stretch together
each preparing for another idle private night,
he says he's almost certainly awake

but sees a galleon in his head, splendid with deities,
dipping its painted open eyes again and again
into the ocean.

Hypnagogia

Insomniacs know better than to lie in bed
unravelling between pyjama seams
or chrysalized in skin too soft or hot or clean,
too loose to occupy, too tight to shed;
they let the world go on without them, windows wide,
dim-cabined aeroplanes fly in one ear
and out the other, sirens twine from far to near,
a taxi stops, drunk women shout good-bye,

someone walks home with change in his pocket, footsteps
out of time with the tick tock of their
meticulous unbroken nightmare, they don't care,
won't wait up listening for sleep to let
itself in like a husband, creep upstairs, apologise
with scratchy cheeks and breath of anaesthetic,
perform the mouth to mouth mental arithmetic
I have been dreaming of with open eyes.

Blackbirds wake themselves up after midnight, will not sing
through car alarms or bitter tit-for-tat
domestics, handbrake turns down well lit cul-de-sacs
but pitch their bounds into the thick pre-morning
loud and clear, reveilles in praise of sleeplessness.
Perched in the upper branches of my head
a reverie descants off key, loses its thread.
My slightest thought can hear itself digress.

The Exercise

Something to talk about besides the rain
at Saturday breakfast, blackbirds dancing
on the colonel my father-in-law's fresh stripes
as he inspects the North Devon Journal Herald
Special Operation Souvenir.
Bacon and eggs. A break in the clouds
and people with mars bars and binoculars
invade the headland. The birdwatchers
have flown away. For every downpour
Baggy Point blossoms again with golf brollies.
Kids get trench-foot playing SAS in the gorse,
pass on vocabulary like a summer cold
until the campsites buzz with expertise.
Soldiers mess up the beach and the sand dunes.
Battleships manoeuvre in the bay –
I leave my clothes in the car
and run through August bank holiday drizzle
to swim with them in water warm and grey
and mineral with the thrill of war.

Casablanca

Time goes by, but in Casablanca
refugees and the free French rise
to Laszlo's fearless *Marseillaise* and Ilsa,

upstairs surprising Rick, still can't unclamp her
hand from the gun, can't pay his asking price,
won't sacrifice one man to save another.

Each year, black memories of tank and panzer
fade to white, the million real lives
lost as Bergman charm and Bogart rancour

silvered screens across America
(a million true tales of do and die)
slip out of focus, fact and fiction blur

until the famous scenes from a Hollywood tearjerker
light up like documentaries in our mind's eye
and war is a theme tune played off-camera

as lovers part, its bittersweet nostalgia
comforting our hearts with queasy rhymes,
its subtext stiff with Allied propaganda.

Watching the plane take off, who would not hanker
for those patriotic days, rewind
to a gin joint on the tip of Africa

where racketeers parade and bankers gather
dinner-jacketed night after night,
or wish for love and glory to remember
when they hear Sam sing *As Time Goes By?*

In the Birchwood

I had always wanted to shoot myself
and so perhaps it was inevitable
that one day I would find a gun in the birchwood,
flick back what I took to be the safety catch
and launch my brain.

The neurons set off immediately
in all directions, reminding me
how often I had needed to be in two places at once,
how I had envied worms their neat ability to divide
and divide again.

Here there and everywhere I lay,
half wishing some part of me
had survived to help with the clearing up afterwards,
or keep an eye on gathering foxes
and frighten the crows.

Although it was odd to be inside out
in such cold weather
a hat would not have made much difference then,
and mine sat upside-down on a tree stump
filling with snow.

Year Off

My brother came back with an amoeba, toe-rings
and a dragon scrolled in flaky indigo across his shoulder.
India, I shrugged, the hippy trail.

He brought me a brass bowl and a stick of teak,
stirred up a sound as slippery and clean as science fiction
or a call to prayer.

Rain swept in smelling of wool and camellias.
He sat on the floor twisting his flip-flops and scratching his head.
We lived like kings. The mountains. God, we got so fucking stoned.

The Playground

I

Two brothers shoot goals
at the edge of the playground
whacking the ball as hard as they can,
looping it catching whacking
and looping all over again
not stopping for breath
or breaking off their commentary
until the older boys turn up
and I take notice
expecting the worst
then glad to be wrong
as the one with the earring says sorry
but can he have his ball back please?
He holds out his hand
and although the brothers can speak
barely a word of English
they understand
their faces shine with it for a moment
making the older boys
shift weight self-consciously
as if ashamed.

II

My daughter can point to an aeroplane
and call it bird.
A helicopter is a bee
a dog a woof.
The woman on the nearby bench
who speaks a language
I can't place
produces an alternative
too small too bouncy
too stinky with dog saliva
found in the bushes
pea-green tennis-ball
which they in turn hold out for my baby.
She has been saying the word for it all afternoon.
The three of them squint in the sunshine.
No one speaks.
Now she has the ball.
Now they can take it back.

March

I promised
once a week to take her
somewhere new

and today it's the playground
over the road
between the tower blocks.

She stands at the lip
of an olympic sandpit
holding out her arms.

I'm thinking
I'll have to shake her out
when we get home

there might be ash
or cat shit in it
broken glass

too fine to see.
Up close the grains shine back
like frozen foam

a stretch of beach
untouched
or rolling inland dunes

no hint of litter or leaf
to say it's not the Sahara
she's asking to try.

I'm wondering
where other children play
if not down here

imagine their mothers
on the fourteenth floor
of Turnpike House

each at her window
watching my toddler
wade across their sand.

Saturday

Gap's dad's rod cost two hundred quid.
Nike brought sandwiches and a scoop of bait in a sweet tin.
They sat on their reflections watching the ducks bugger off
and bankers in flats get out of bed.

We had a shark on holiday, said Gap.
Nike did target practice on the lilypads
and a couple of girls came by to look at the maggots.

If I lived here I'd piss off my balcony straight in the canal,
                                        said Gap from
the back of the old electricity hut.
One flick and the rod was a light-sabre,
a trick Nike had been working on all afternoon.
They stood on the towpath listening to tiddlers and gnats
as the sun went down and the girls came back from the
                                        shopping centre
with their jeans in a carrier bag.
                        We caught a cat, said Gap,
and Nike and the rod became a car-park barrier,
the kind no one can pass for less than cash.

Highbury Pool

She climbs to the top of the elephant slide
and bends one knee, looks down, then catches my eye
and smiles as pee spatters her ankles. Outside
it's trying to snow, but the pool is a frenzy
of wallowing hot children. Chewed floats lap
at the steps where mothers bask and babies cling
blissfully. Ten minutes ago I hoped
she'd dare follow me in, timid and shivering
in last summer's swimsuit, its kingfisher blue
all that distinguishes her, now, from the next
drenched toddler. One day, I suppose,
I'll have to choose which clothes recall the best
of these years, folded forgotten things I'd rather lose
than give away. She waves, then sits, lets go.

Natural History

Little enough to walk straight under the turnstile
and sashay gleefully out of sight, her yellow coat
flashing through pushchairs and arches, winking good-bye
to the throng while I pocket my change, call out,

she does not stop to look at a thing
until we reach the piped cicada and birdsong paradise
of polystyrene crag and spot-lit vegetation
where lizard-hipped dinosaurs

guzzle their catch, dip animated heads to feed in turn
from its fat throat, slashed flank and belly.
I want to go, she wants to stay, explains
those little ones there are kissing their mummy.

Crying

They cry because they're babies, babies cry –
they're hungry, uncomfortable, need to sleep
or sometimes for no reason you or I

however anxiously we empathise
can guess, or for no reason but to keep
us guessing night and day, they cry and cry.

They stand up, learn to walk and talk and tie
their shoelaces. You watch them cross the street
without holding hands, but sometimes I

fall over at school, half-strangled, as they fight
for one more last good-bye; and let them weep
when I am not at liberty to cry.

Their swollen soft distracted faces dry.
Mine is forgotten. Free to drag my feet
unsupervised back through the playground, I

will be late for work, but sometimes stop to spy
on them, or in a flash of childish pique
call out their names, want them to see me cry,
their fat transparent tears escape my eyes.

January

I love a cold snap,
the way it marches in from Canada
or the Baltic, almost but never
exactly as the weather-map predicts.
The way it might make everything go wrong
cheers people up. Ice on the roads
is an excuse to eat more chocolate,
or lie in the bath imagining I am a Japanese macaque
chin-deep in volcano water,
dizzy beneath my hat of snow.
I love the way it makes me want to ring my aunts
pretending to thank them for Christmas.
Granny will be too proud to claim
her heating allowance again this year
and she complains about the snow,
which never lasts long in Lyme Regis
and is nothing like the Welsh snow of her youth.
We are still waiting for it here.
The city farm cock crows into Paradise Park,
and boys outside the pupil referral unit
lust after mopeds as usual.
I watch the sky, but darkness falls
unaccompanied and the girls are drinking their milk
when you ring from a blizzard in Moorgate
to tell me your bus is stuck.
You laugh at us for being last to know
and listen as I pull up the blinds
and send them out in pyjamas and coats, our garden
beautiful in the sky's bright brown,
our children walking like astronauts
through freshly frozen tea.

Ice

A superstition I have invented, living here,
says the canal must freeze
each winter.

When it does
I want to stand with the boys on the towpath
chucking things

to see if they will slide,
how far,
if they will break the ice.

A stick, a coke can, half a brick
all skitter down the slab in the lock
so now we have to know

how thick is it, exactly,
and how quickly
would we need to run?

Who wants to be James Bond
crossing the swamp
in *Live and Let Die?*

Who's lightest?
Where have the ducks
and alligators gone?

Hand Car Wash

Men of all ages
vacuuming sweets
from minicab ashtrays
wet through their overalls
wringing out rags
their faces the faces
of bob-a-job boys
on a cul-de-sac drive
in the long summer holiday
under their eyelashes
waiting for someone
to flick the first sud.

Names

They like their names. The longer you call
the longer they will sit on their beds
at one with the sound of their own importance
not coming down for tea, not listening
to what you say about the temperature of eggs
or what children in Africa eat,
how but for you they could have been sent home
with somebody else's little white hospital bracelet,
hot in an extra layer of syllables.

How cosy it was before you had to call them anything,
before their names came into their own,
appearing on bus-tickets and shopping lists,
at four or five their shaky signatures
transforming scribbles into art,
your kitchen cluttered with scrap-paper autographs,
on felt tip pens their names in gold
a trademark of superior quality,
before their names went out into the world
to make a name for themselves on application forms,
settling on desks in the Passport Office or the DSS
as alphabetical dust.

Back through the letterbox they swing
like unrepentant runaways
sent home with the tale of their own adventure,
calling your children, filling their heads
with dreams of a better life somewhere else.
In permanent ink you mark their names
on the necks of this year's anoraks
and hope they will be warm enough

walking away from your idea of "Mae" or "William" –
their name and the name you christened them
as different, now, as twins
who hang about by the coat pegs at school
and smile through Register whispering
Be my friend?

Wishes

I wish I could somehow fast-forward you,
skip through the future to whichever year
I fancy, stop where I will, and get to know
some other you, a different kind of man
each time, fall in and out of love
and so keep moving on but still stay true.

The glamour of older men, it's true,
never attracted me. When I met you
I thought we'd uncover the arts of love
together, assumed our equal years
equalled identical desires, looked for no man
to teach me what to do. But now I know

I wish you could be someone I don't know,
someone who won't expect me to be true
to myself, eternally the woman
I seem to become when I'm with you.
Be forty-five, say, and me not one year
older than I am today, free of love

and weak-kneed with the thrill of making love
in a doorway with someone I know
I shouldn't be. I want you the year
you go grey, to see you losing love's true
shape, your muscles waste, and the skin hang off you
like soft paper. My dirty old man

how badly you'll want a young woman
like me, a honey, to stay and love
and look after you then. People will think you
a man among men, imagine you must know
what women want. If it were true
I would grow old with you and let each year

write itself on my face, forget the year
we met, when you were nobody's man
but your own: untried, untested, true,
a young man who believed in true love
in love with a woman too young to know
what she believed. Now I believe in you.

And you, what do you see in me year after year?
Someone you already know, a woman
worn out by love, or a wish come true?

Dalby Bush Farm

Acres of water-logged, half-frozen furrow tinged with winter wheat.
Ewes in the beet field. Mice in the wardrobes. Flies in the mice.
Left-over motorway biscuits for tea with Lapsang Souchong
by a leaky dimplex. Located, my cot in the stable beyond repair.

At dusk we shivered into boots determined to have what we came for
and walked together, pigeon-stepping through the clogged earth,
showing you hedge-rows, ditches and rusty gates,
the branches of trees we love.
                         It was the hour for deer.
Drenched heads shuddering at the edge of the pine plantation
watched our white umbrella ghost through the downpour.

Acknowledgements

Acknowledgements are due to the editors of the following publications where some of these poems first appeared: *Poetry Review, Smith's Knoll, Magma, New Welsh Review* and *The Rialto.*

I would like to thank The Author's Foundation for a grant in 2003, and Colin Falck and Greta Stoddard for their notes on the manuscript.